THE HUMONGOUS PUSHKA
IN THE SKY

by

DANNY SIEGEL
Author of *Tell Me A Mitzvah* and *After The Rain*

Illustrated by
GARTH POTTS

THE TOWN HOUSE PRESS
Pittsboro, North Carolina

GARTH POTTS, the illustrator of this book, is the Executive Director of the Birmingham Jewish Community Center. He has an MFA from Oklahoma and says that he would like to have become a sports cartoonist. This comes close. In his "spare time," he and his wife, Marilynn, are parents of four children: Shoshana, Micah, Gabriel and Zachary, each of whom insisted upon reviewing and approving their father's handiwork on these pages.

DEDICATION

For Rabbi Harold Schulweis
Professors Gerald Bubis, Elliot Dorff and Ron Wolfson
and
Merrill Alpert and Laura Kaplansky
My Teachers
Rebbis in the Ways of Menschlichkeit

Copyright © 1993 by Danny Siegel. All rights reserved.
Library of Congress Catalogue Card Number 93-61454
International Standard Book Number: 0-940653-36-2

Printed in the United States of America

You might be walking home from the school bus and just happen to look up for a minute.

Or before you go to bed at night, you might look out the window at the moon and the stars

Or if it is summer and
there is a thunderstorm,
you might want
to see what patterns
the lightning is making.

Sometimes when you look
at the sky in the daytime,
you see clouds and try
to guess what shapes they are.

You might see a big hand
or a car or a tree top or two
or a sheep.
It all depends on the clouds
that day and how much
you let your mind make
pictures out of them.

At night you do the same thing with the stars.

You start connecting
the dots all across the sky
and come up with
a dragon or a kite

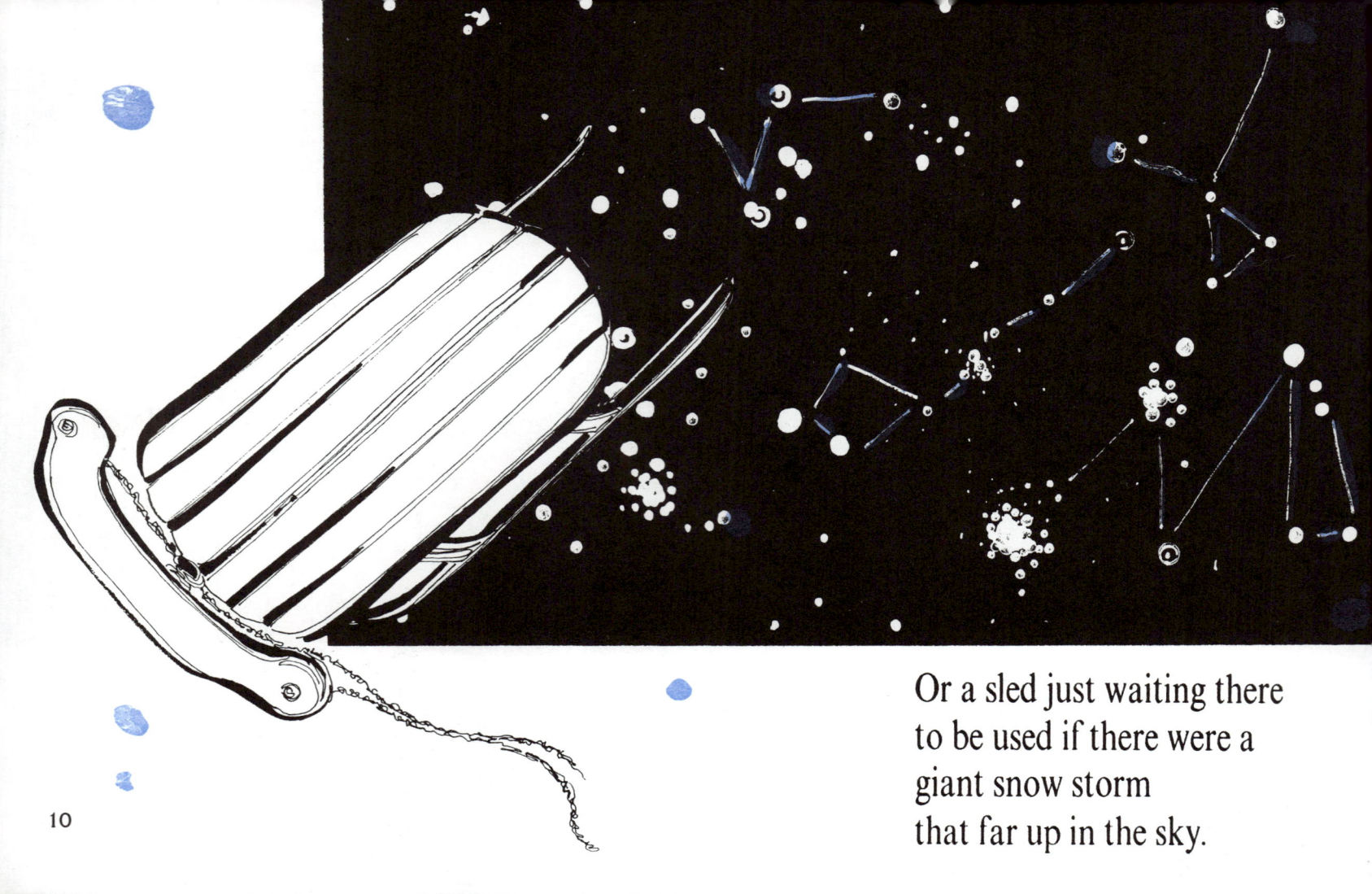

Or a sled just waiting there
to be used if there were a
giant snow storm
that far up in the sky.

I suppose it would be hard to picture fifty-six strings of spaghetti piled high in a bowl, though you could, if you use your imagination.

You might even see a miniature golf course up there or a frozen yogurt store with nine flavors. But that depends on the stars and your eyes and how much you use your imagination.

For thousands of years
people have been coming up
with star pictures
and giving them names.
In fact, scientists have eighty-eight
official star pictures they call
constellations, and each one has
a fancy name and a regular name.
If you look at a list of the
eighty-eight star pictures,
you'll find many animals.

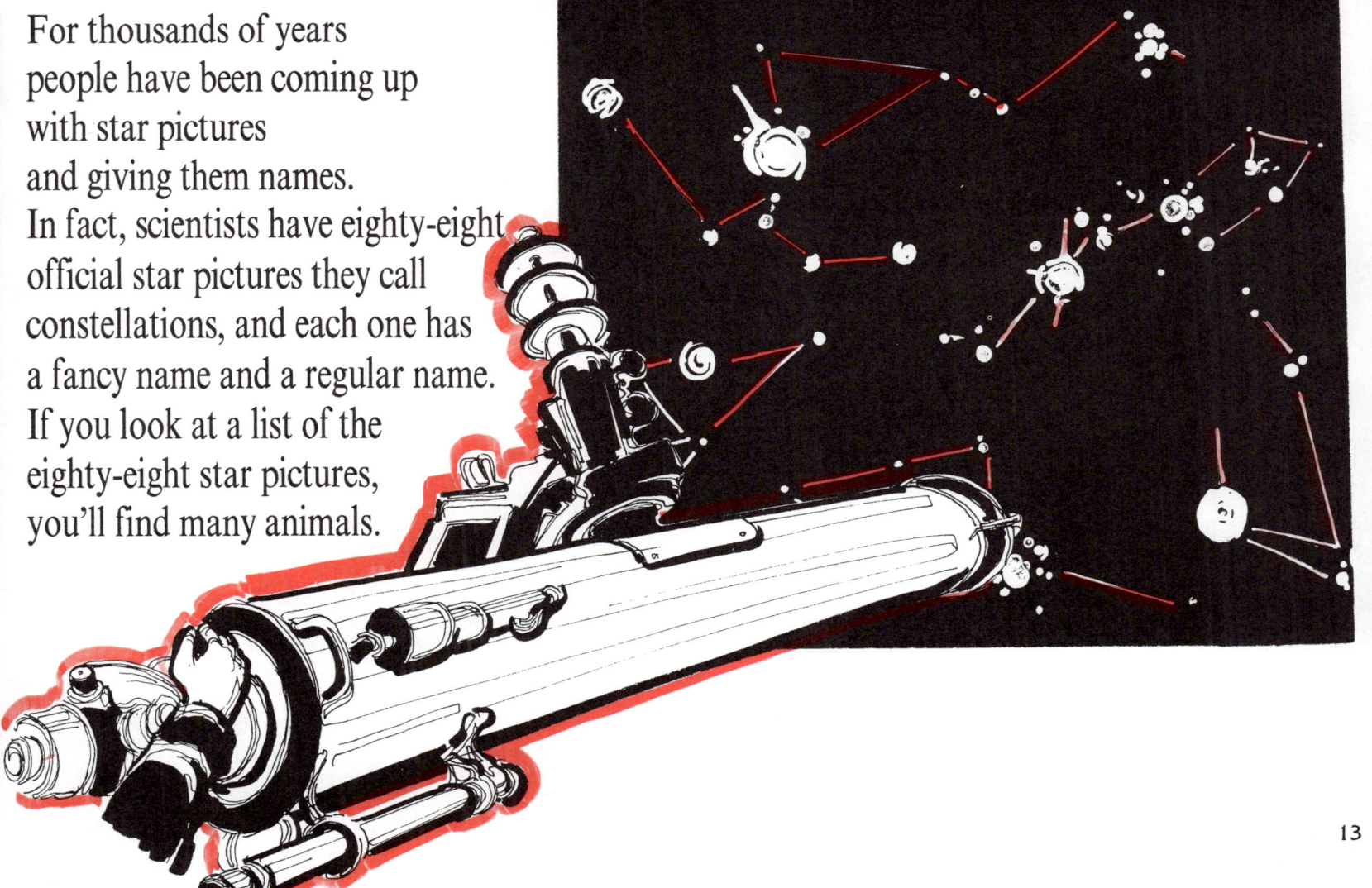

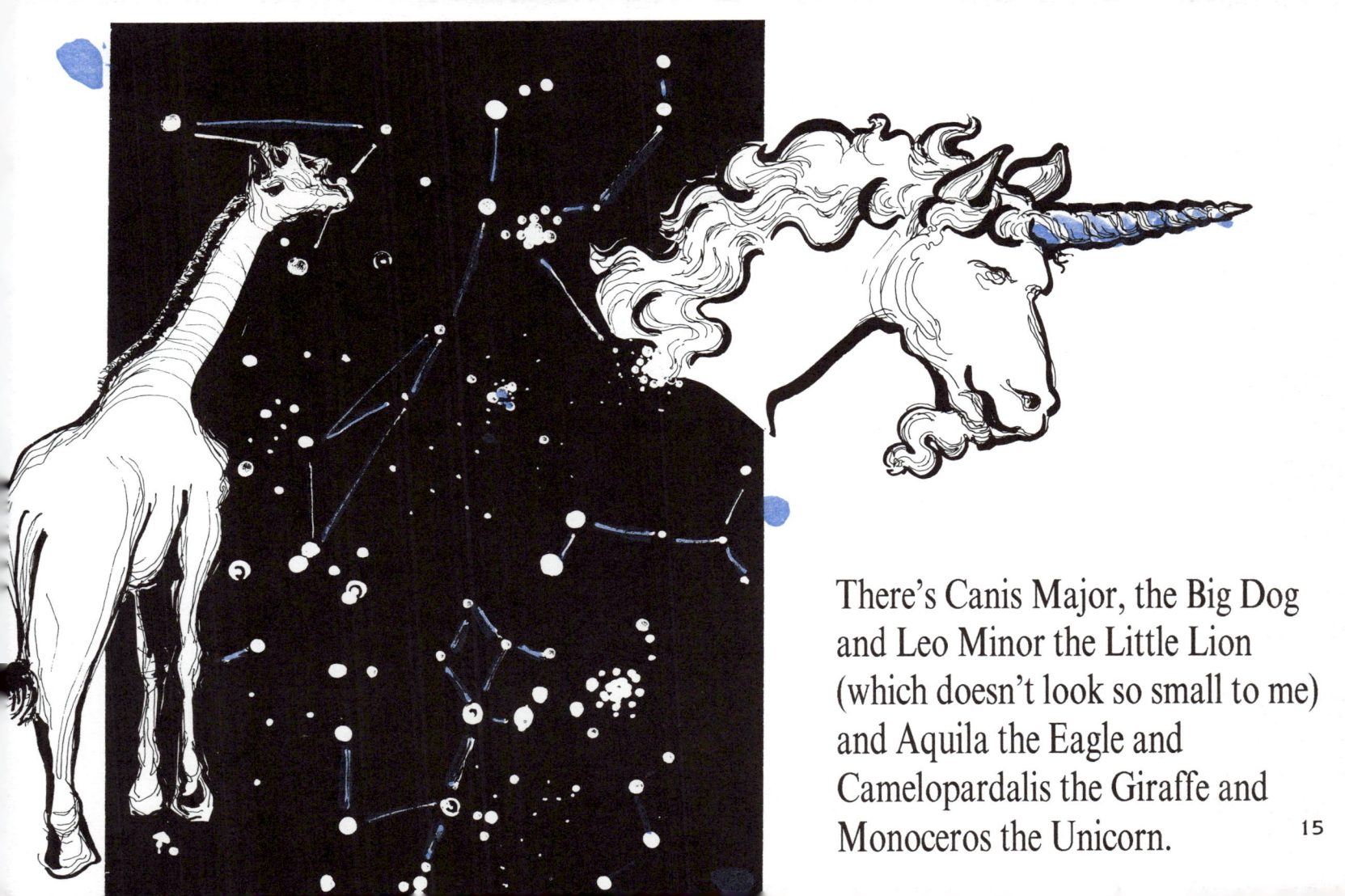

There's Canis Major, the Big Dog
and Leo Minor the Little Lion
(which doesn't look so small to me)
and Aquila the Eagle and
Camelopardalis the Giraffe and
Monoceros the Unicorn.

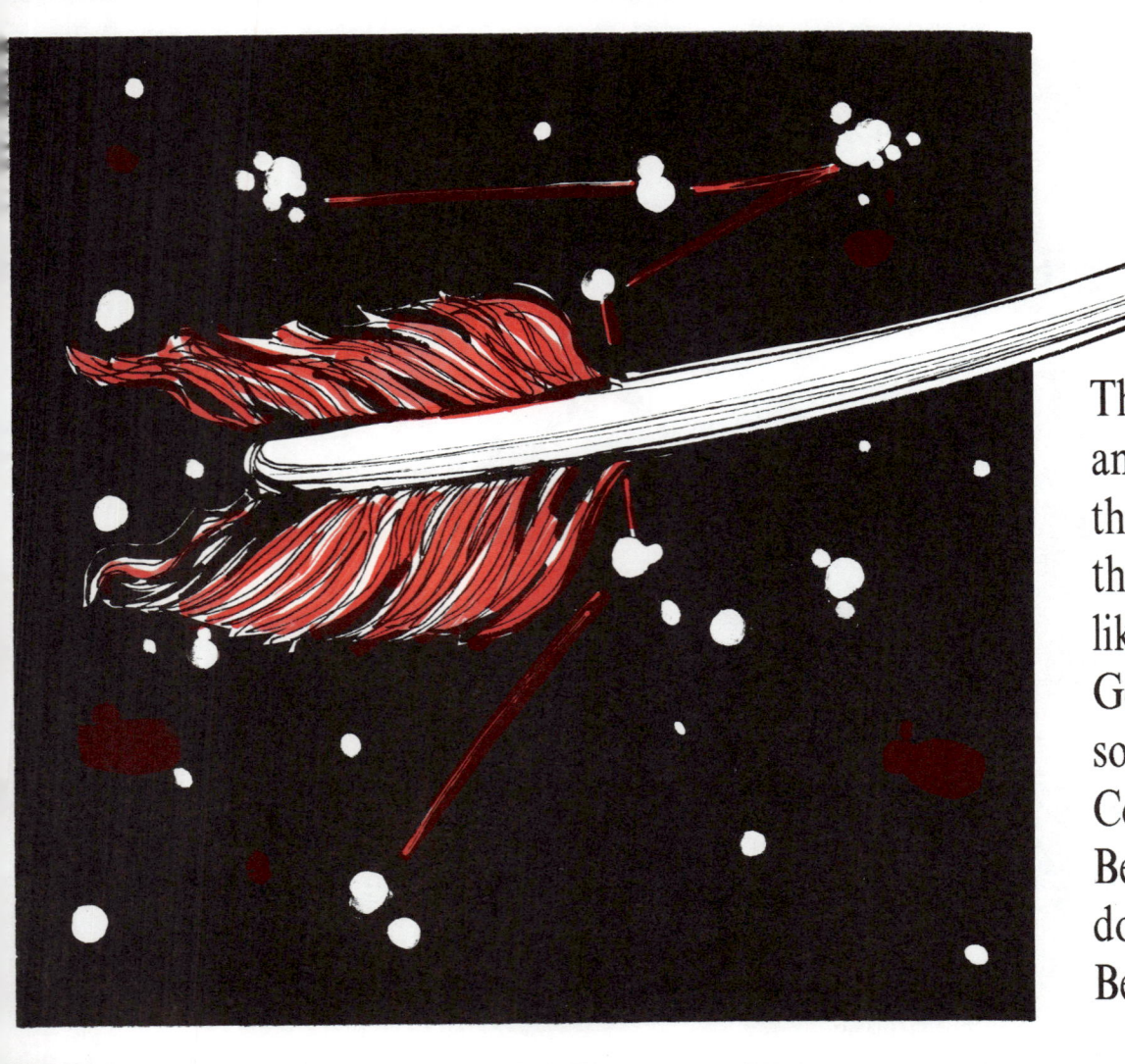

They're not all animals, of course
and I can't list them all -
though I could add a few
that aren't animals,
like Sagitta the Arrow and
Gemini the Twins and
something strange like
Coma Berenices, which means
Berenice's Hair, though I
don't have any idea who this
Berenice was.

16

And of course, we can't forget
Ursa Major the Big Bear
which has inside of it that
enormous, deep spoon called
the Big Dipper.
And those are only *some*
of the star pictures, at least
some of the famous ones on the
official list.
Daytime or night there's something
new you can do with your
imagination if you just stretch it a little

Some morning, when you see the clouds, if, as best as you can tell, there's a very large sheep in the sky, you can picture using the wool to make a sweater to keep someone warm.

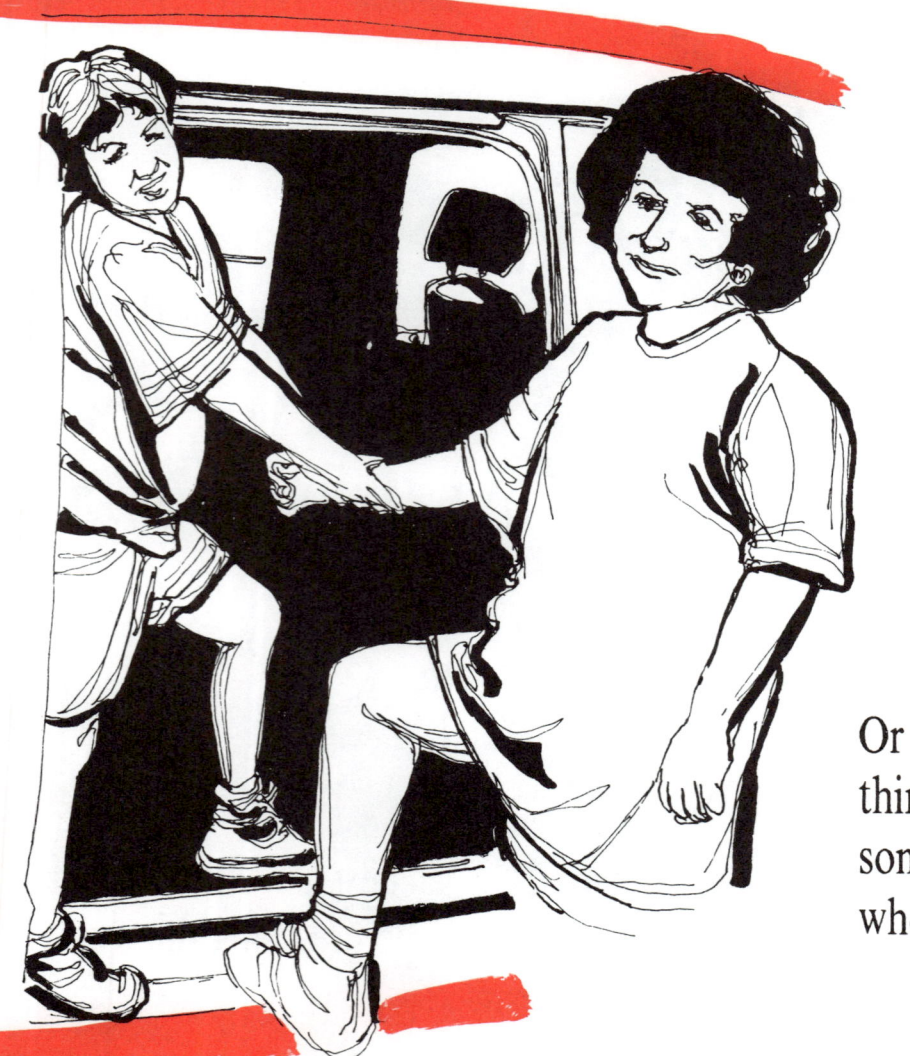

Or if it is a car you saw,
think of how you could ask
someone to drive another person
who lives all alone out to a picnic

Or to an amusement park

Or circus.

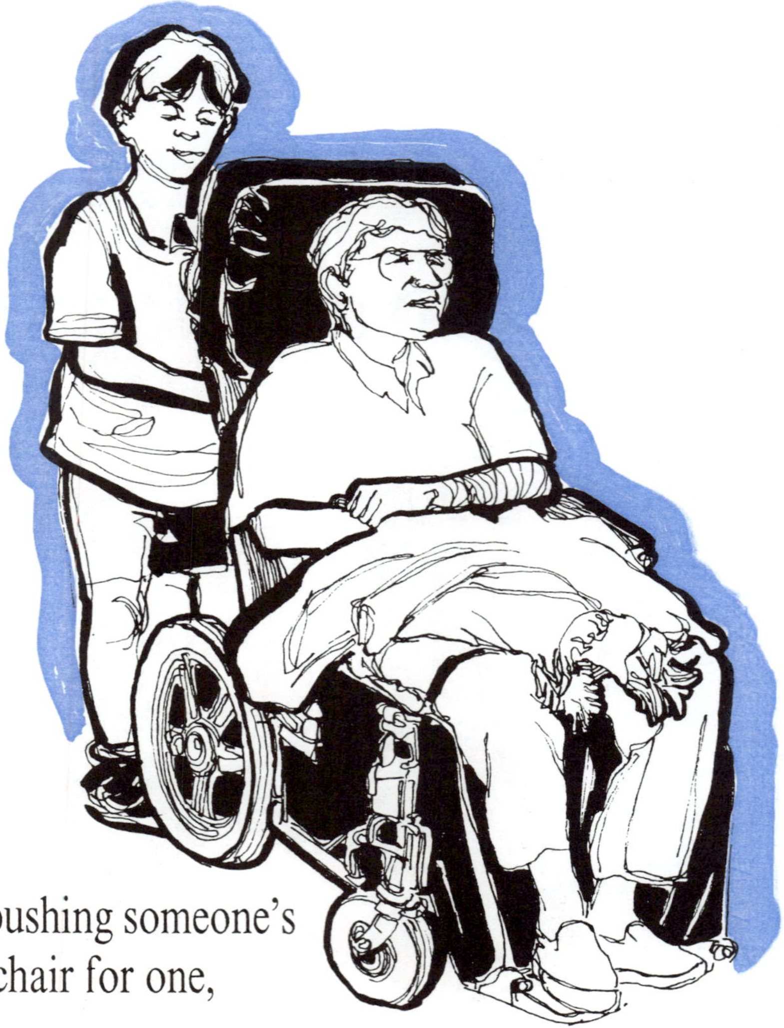

And a hand --- well, that's easy. There's at least as many ways to use your hands for Mitzvahs as there are clouds.

Like pushing someone's wheelchair for one,

Or pointing to the words in a book when you are helping someone to learn how to read.

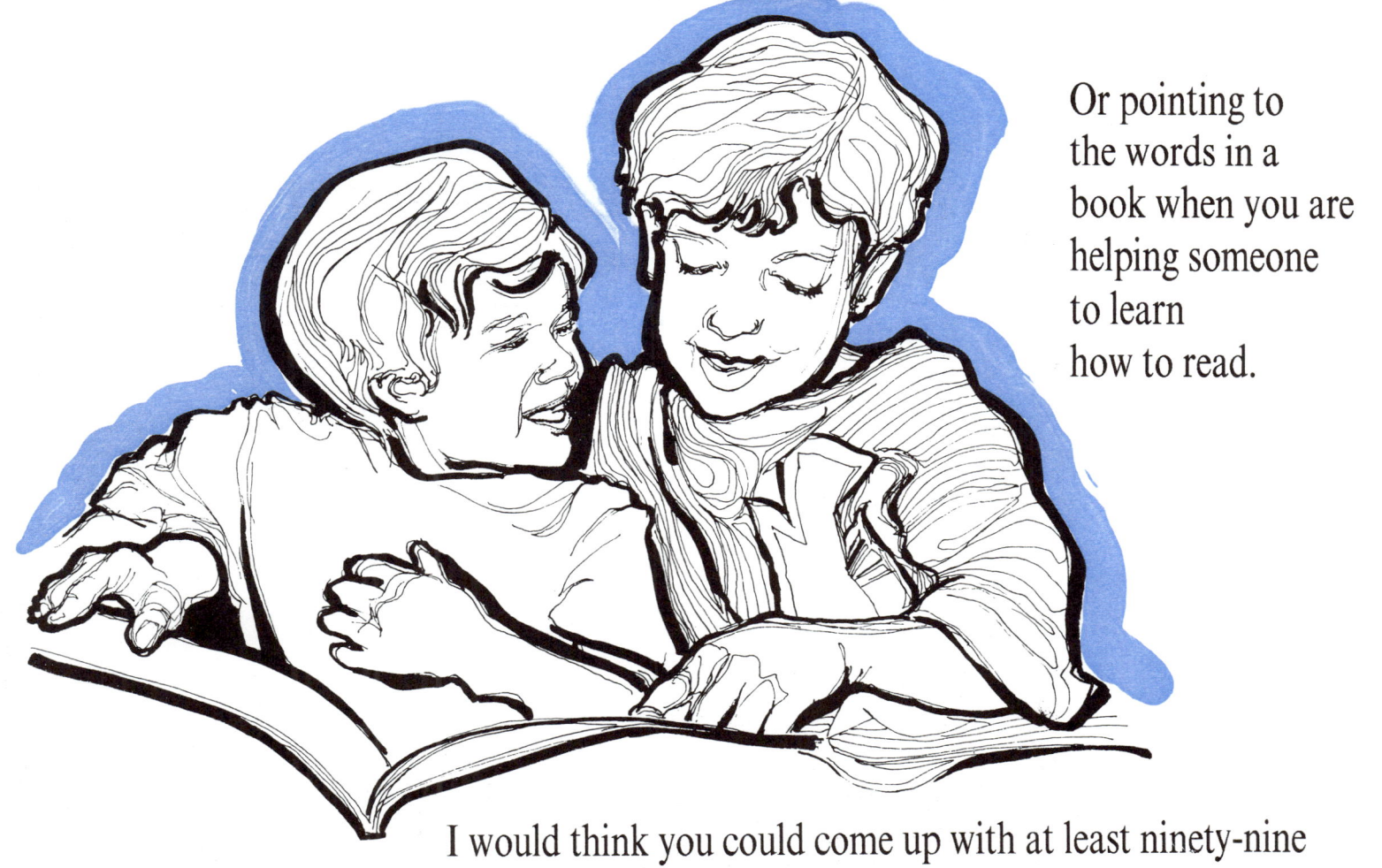

I would think you could come up with at least ninety-nine other ways to use that hand or your own hand with Mitzvahs.

And at night---
well, you can come up with just about anything, because there are so many stars in the sky that look like dots

just waiting for you to connect them to each other.

That dragon in the sky...
you can imagine a big stuffed dragon
you could take to the hospital
for other children
so they can have some fun
until they get better.

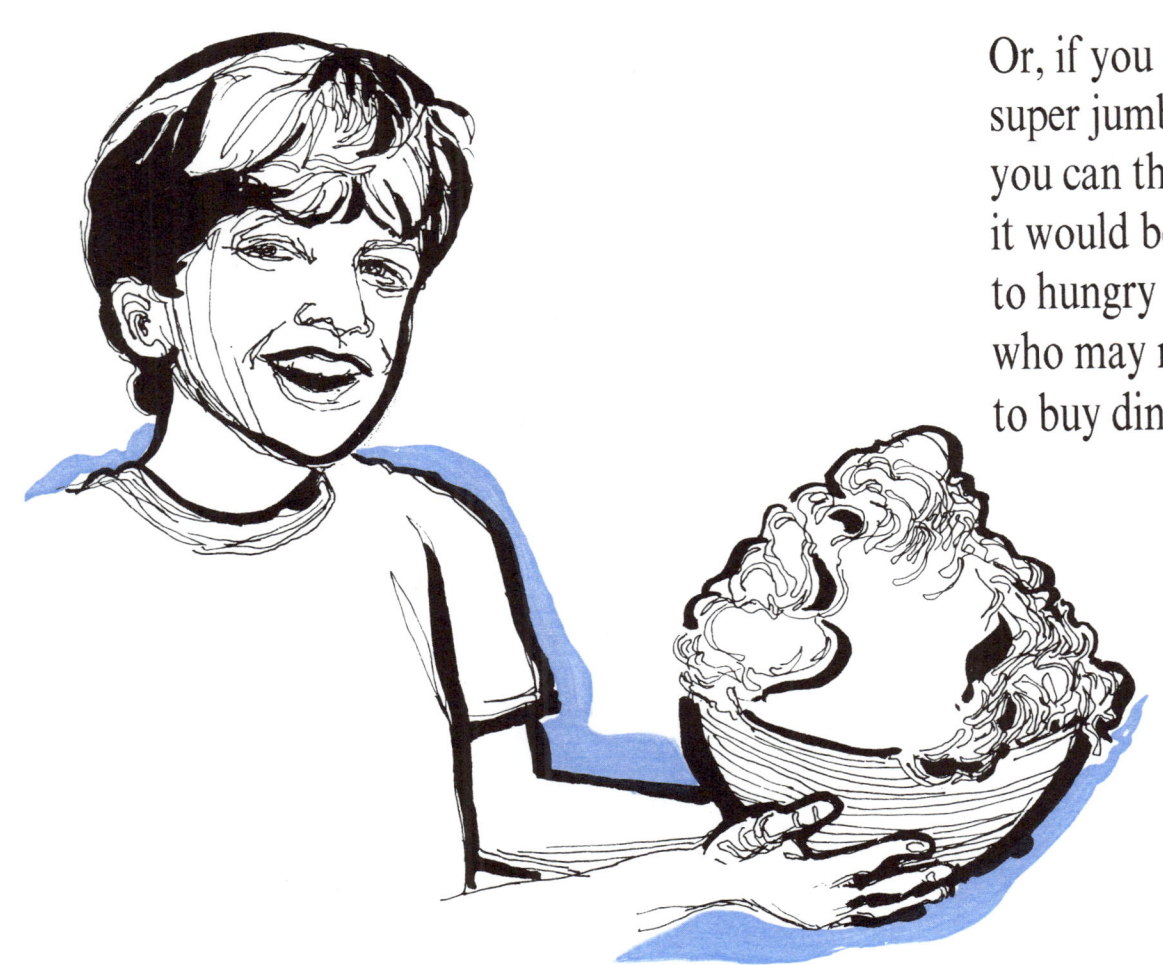

Or, if you found that
super jumbo portion of spaghetti,
you can think how good
it would be to get some more food
to hungry people
who may not have enough money
to buy dinner.

And the frozen yogurt would make a nice dessert.

You might even see
Ursa Major the Big Bear
and figure out six ways
to get teddy bears to
children who
don't have them.

There's just no end to what you can see up there at night.

You might even find a humongous pushka in the sky, one that could be filled with so much Tzedakah money everyone in the world would be happy.

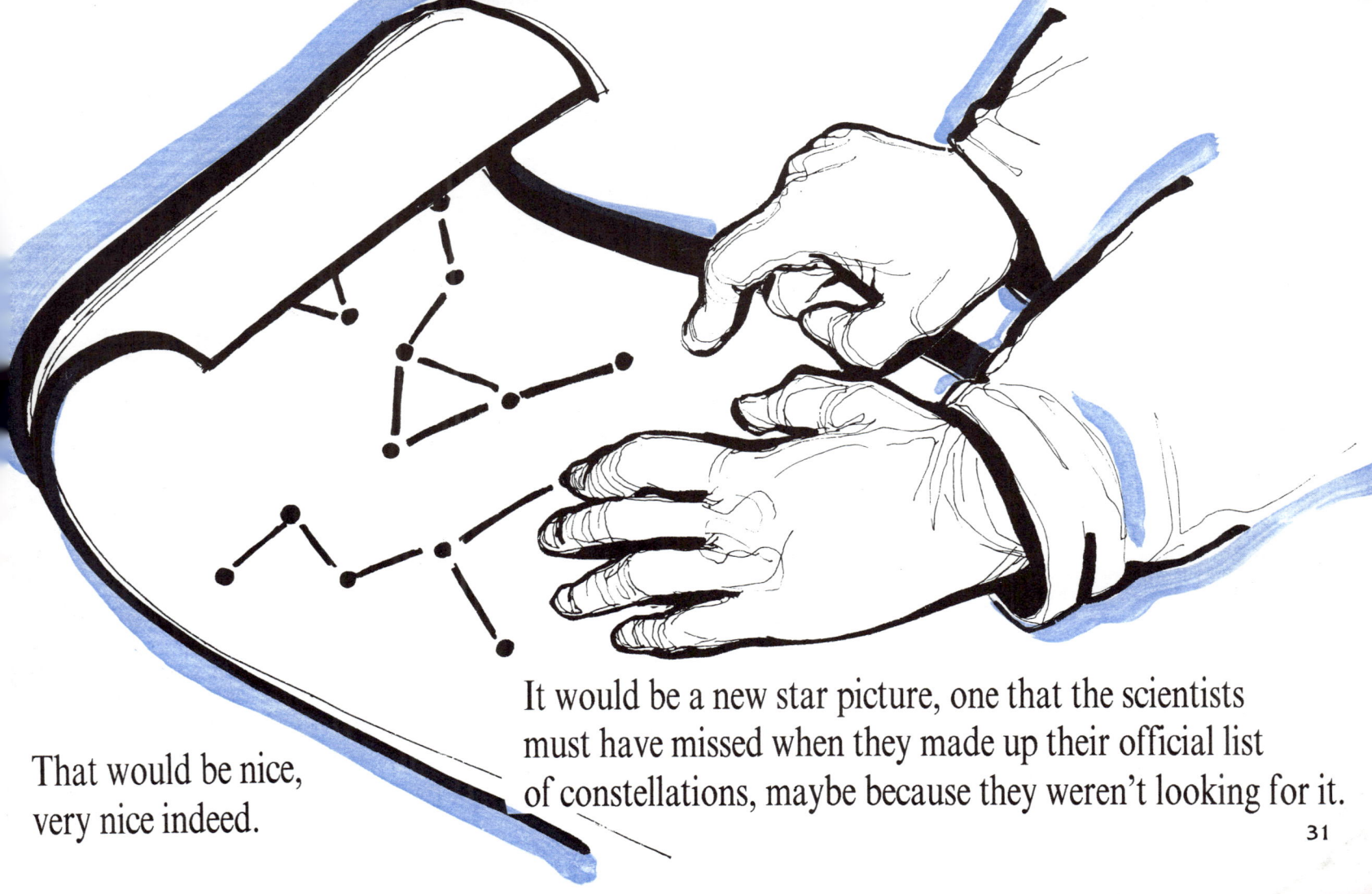

That would be nice, very nice indeed.

It would be a new star picture, one that the scientists must have missed when they made up their official list of constellations, maybe because they weren't looking for it.

Just remember--- the next time you look up at the stars at night, look all over the sky and see if you can find that humongous pushka.